Jazz Guitar Christmas

Fun and challenging arrangements of 13 Christmas favorites
in both easy and intermediate *chord melody* style
by George Ports

Cover photo of a Kenny Burrell prototype
guitar (serial # 41798) made by Bob Benedetto,
courtesy of Bob and Cindy Benedetto

Cover art by **Shawn Brown**
Cover Photo by **John Bender**
Paste-up by **Ken Warfield**
Music Notation by **George Ports**
Layout/Production by **Ron Middlebrook**

ISBN 1-57424-063-3
SAN 683-8022

Table Of Contents

About The Author

Raised in southwest Los Angeles, George Ports began playing the violin at 8 years, clarinet at age 10, and trumpet at age 12. His musical ability, was instilled by his parents, who were also musically inclined. His father, Eugene Ports, played for the Los Angeles Symphony Orchestra as 1st chair clarinet, and clarinet in the U.S. Naval Orchestra. His mother, Esther Ports, was a concert pianist who was asked to sing for the Metropolitan Opera. He continued his musical interests in these various instruments until age 20, when he began playing guitar. George has been fortunate in that he has studied with the "greats" who have influenced him the most, such as: *Barney Kessel, Howard Roberts, Irving Ashby,* and *Herman Mitchell.* Others he has studied from include: *Jimmy Wyble, Irv Mayhew, Pat McKee, Don Mock, Ron Eschete,* and *Les Wise.* George has also benefited from attending seminars by various well-known artists including: *Larry Carlton, Pat Metheny, Joe Diorio, Joe Pass, Ted Greene, Herb Ellis, Jerry Hahn,* and *Tommy Tedesco.*

During the early '60's, while continuing with his studies in music, George played with many local rock groups. For the following 12 years he traveled with Las Vegas-type show groups across the nation. Some of these groups, well known on the circuit as, *"Hot Pants-Old Hats Review,"* with *Red Coffee,* the voice of *"Yacky Doodle Duck,"* the cartoon character; *Curtis and Vader* comedy team; and *Chasers Four,* the warmup group for *Rowan and Martin* from the T.V. show, *"Laugh-In."*

While with the group *"Hi-Hats,"* he wrote and recorded *"Creepy"* on the Hi-Hat label, and while with *"Outrageous 4+1,"* he recorded *"Unchained Melody"* and *"Psycho,"* on the Spec label. George was on the recording session for the title track of the movie, *"Bad Georgia Road."*

George was a member of the second graduating class of Guitar Institute of Technology, (G.I.T.), where he was awarded the Certificate of Merit for *"Continuous Outstanding Performance."* He has written the music calligraphy for over 30 music books for such authors as *Howard Roberts, Chuck Rainey,* and *Les Wise,* to mention just a few.

George has been teaching all types of music, including jazz, for the past 36 years. He has been teaching at Patrick's Music School, in Fullerton, California, since 1980.

All Through The Night

(Easy)

Moderately

arr. by George Ports

All Through The Night

(Intermediate)

Moderately

arr. by George Ports

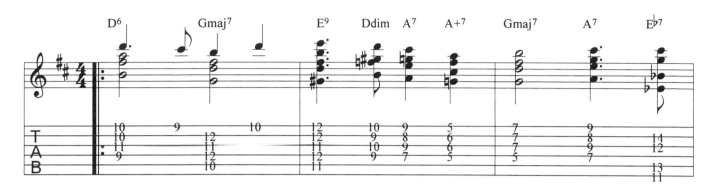

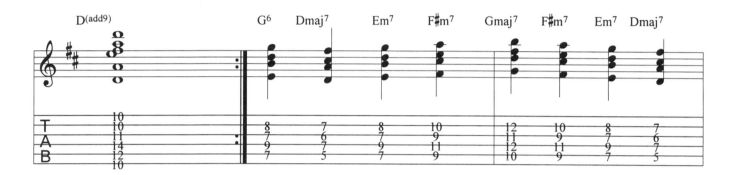

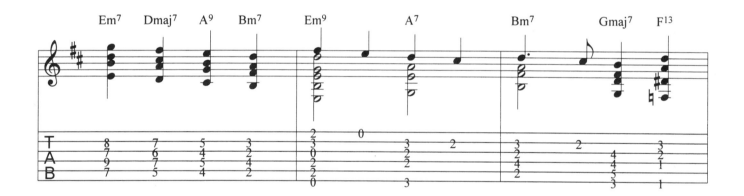

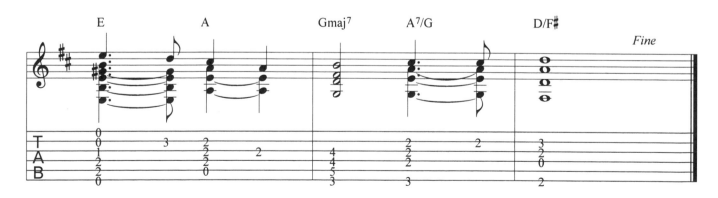

Angels From The Realm Of Glory

(Easy)

Stately

arr. by George Ports

Angels From The Realm Of Glory

(Intermediate)

arr. by George Ports

Tap with right index

Away In A Manger

(Easy)

Gently

arr. by George Ports

Away In A Manger

(Intermediate)

Gently

arr. by George Ports

9

The Boar's Head Carol

(Easy)

Freely

arr. by George Ports

The Boar's Head Carol

(Intermediate)

Freely

arr. by George Ports

The Coventry Carol

(Easy)

Gently

arr. by George Ports

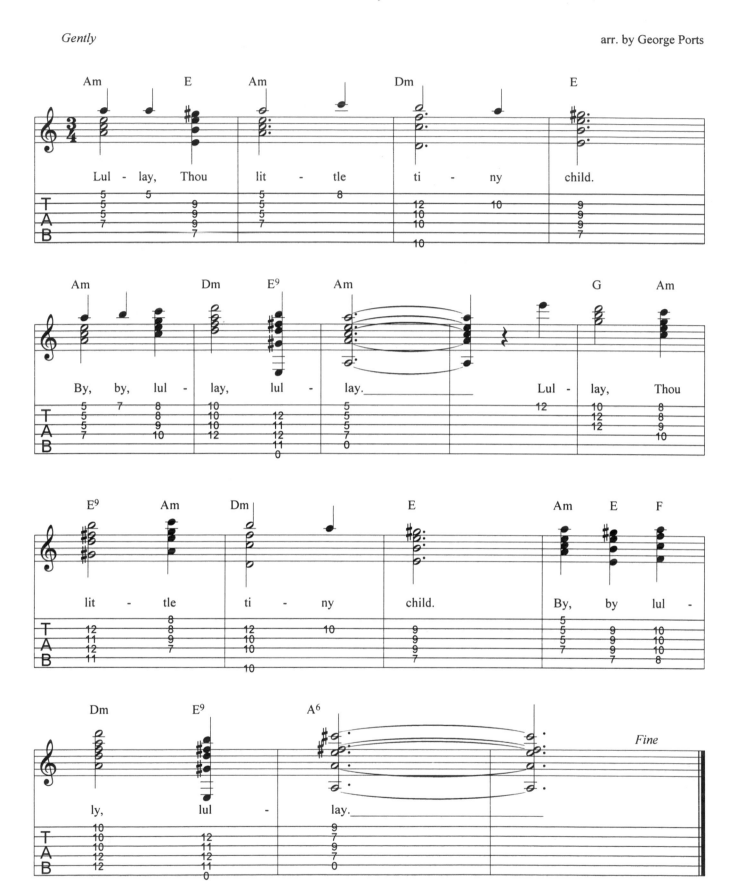

The Coventry Carol

(Intermediate)

Gently

arr. by George Ports

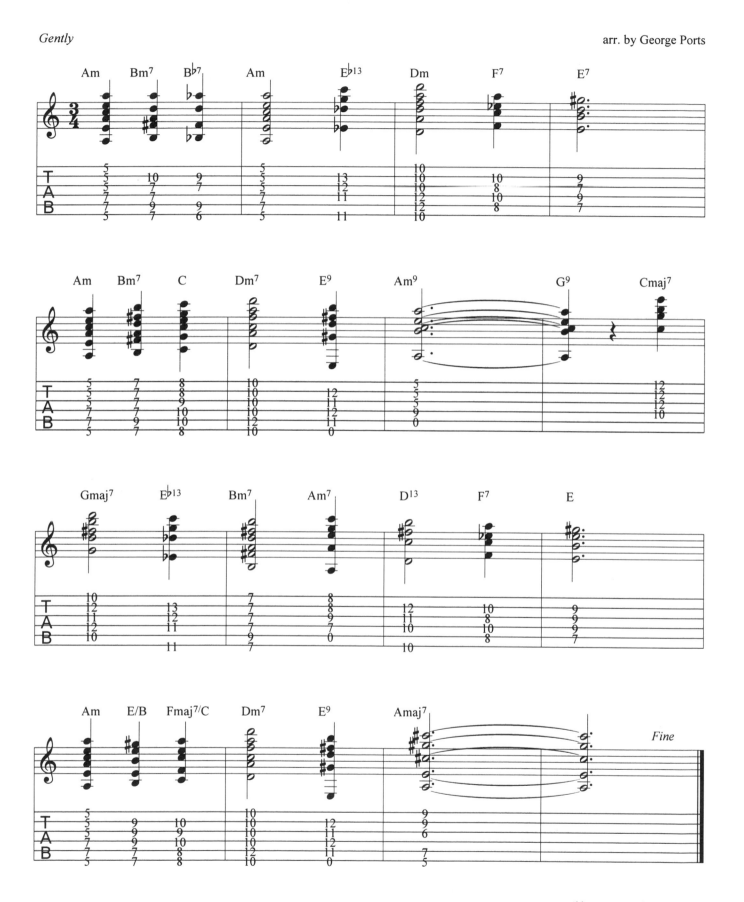

Deck The Halls

(Easy)

Brightly

arr. by George Ports

Deck The Halls

(Intermediate)

Brightly

arr. by George Ports

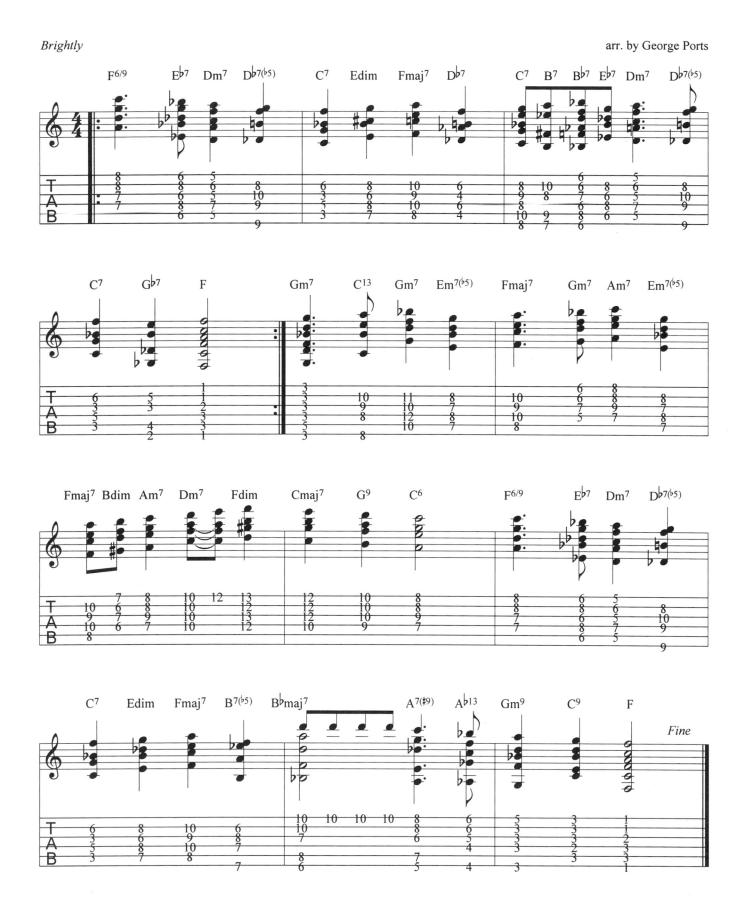

The Friendly Beast

(Easy)

Moderately

arr. by George Ports

The Friendly Beast

(Intermediate)

Moderately

arr. by George Ports

From The Eastern Mountains

(Easy)

Hymn-like

arr. by George Ports

From The Eastern Mountains

(Intermediate)

Hymn

arr. by George Ports

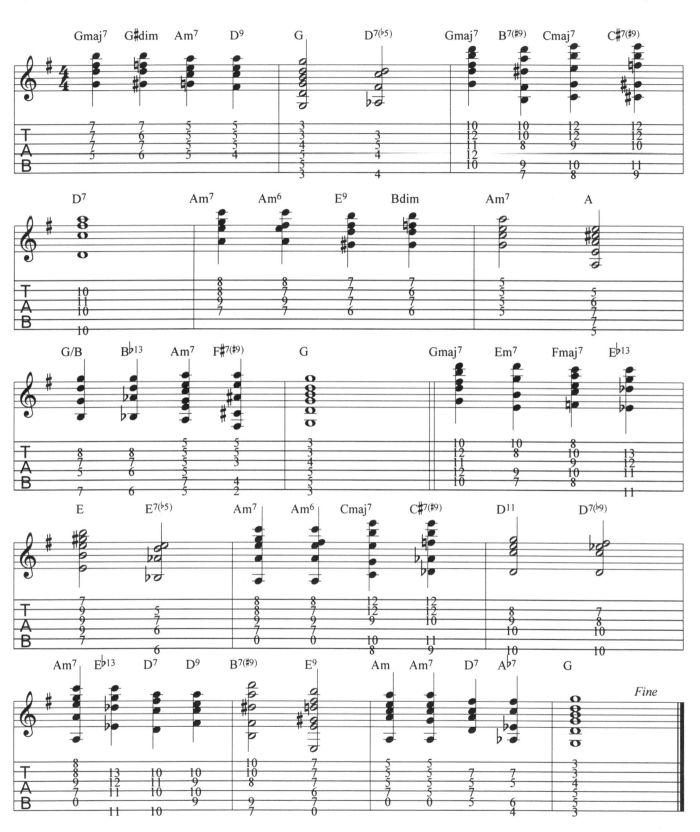

Jolly Old St. Nicholas

(Easy)

Moderately

arr. by George Ports

Jolly Old St. Nicholas

(Intermediate)

Moderately

arr. by George Ports

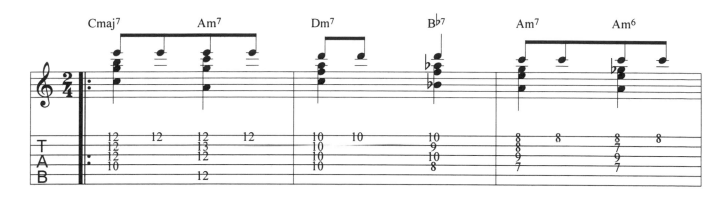

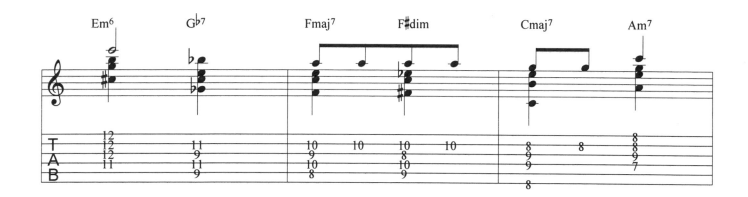

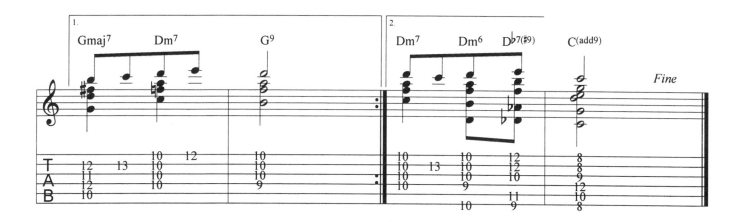

O' Bethlehem

(Easy)

Slowly

arr. by George Ports

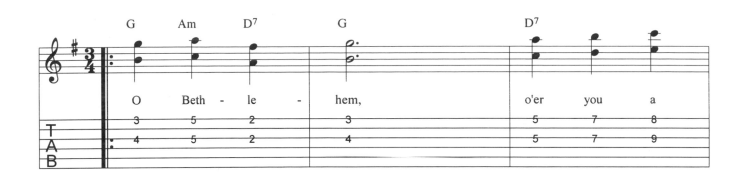

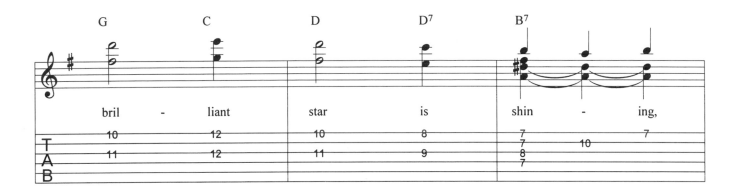

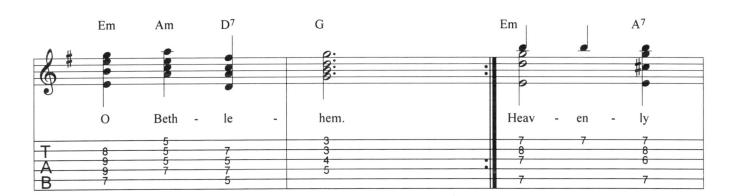

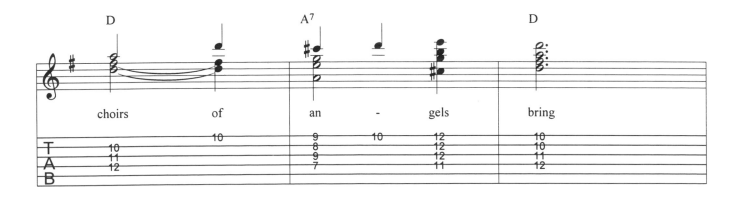

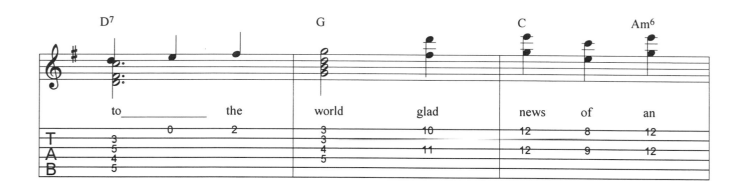

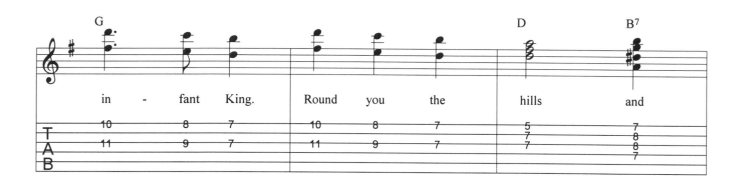

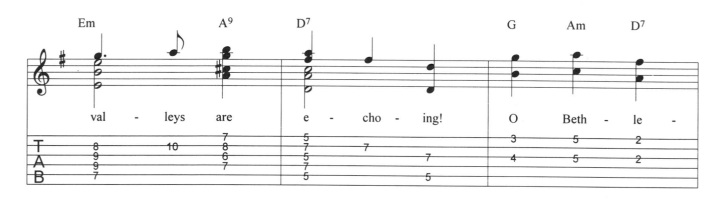

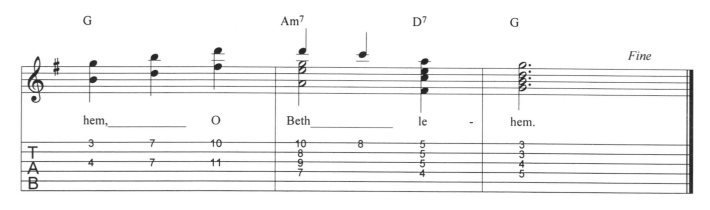

O' Bethlehem

(Intermediate)

Slowly

arr. by George Ports

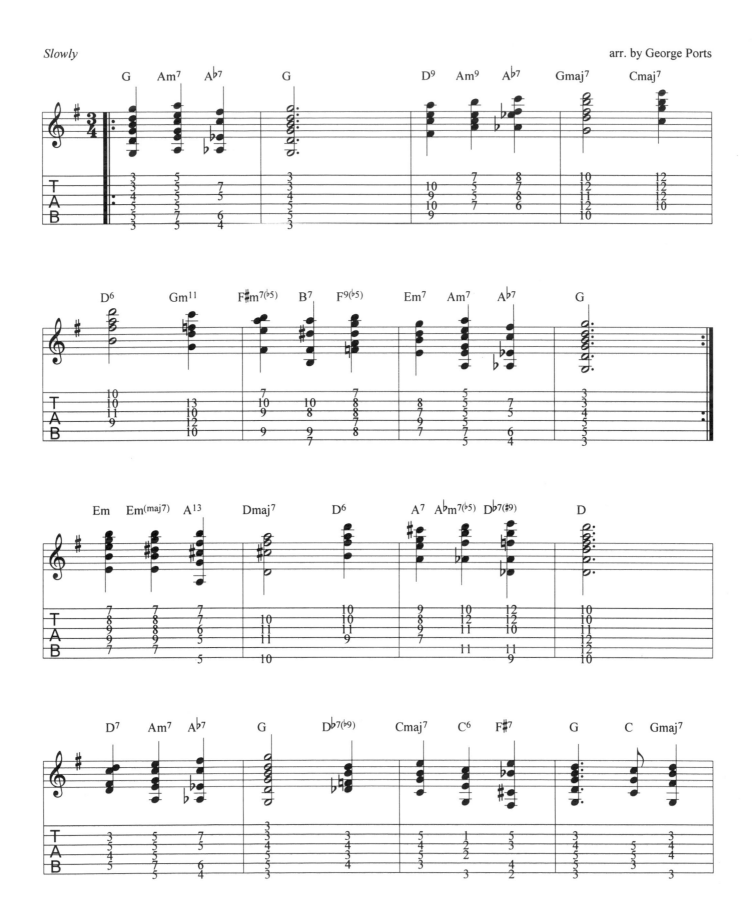

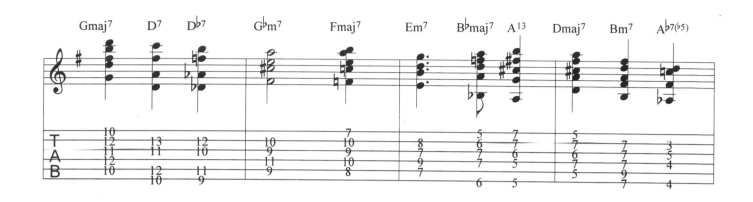

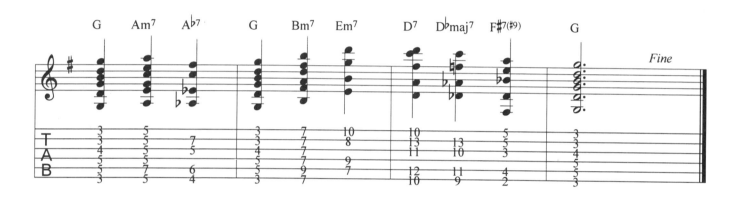

HOW LONG TO KEEP THE CHRISTMAS TREE: A VISUAL GUIDE

O' Christmas Tree

(Easy)

Moderately

arr. by George Ports

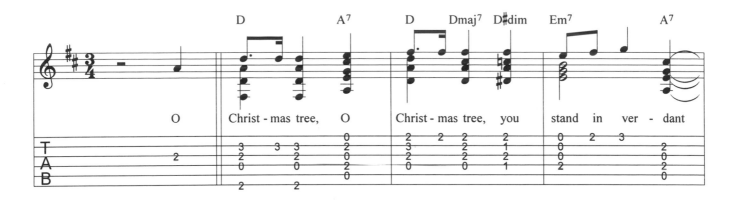

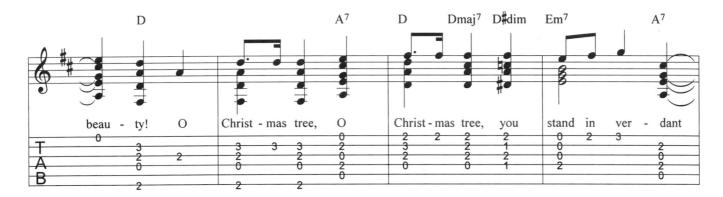

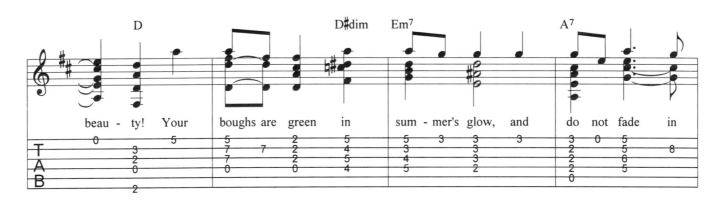

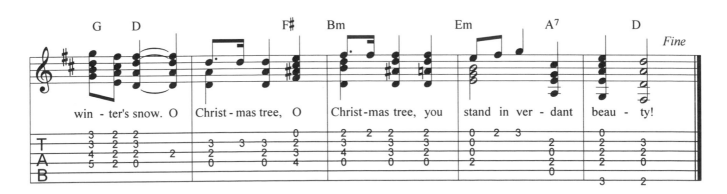

O' Christmas Tree

(Intermediate)

Moderately

arr. by George Ports

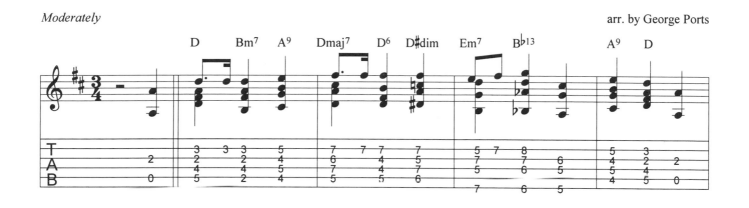

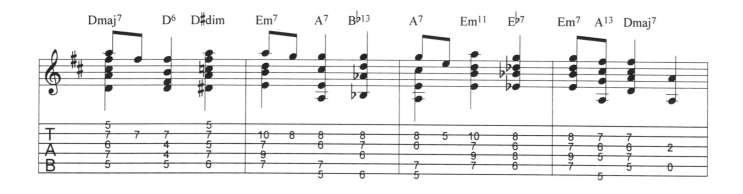

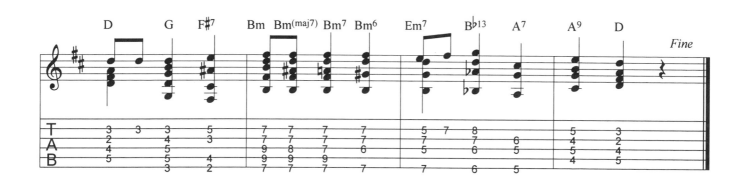

this arrangement
copyright 1998 by Centerstream Publishing

Sleep Holy Babe

(Easy)

Quietly

arr. by George Ports

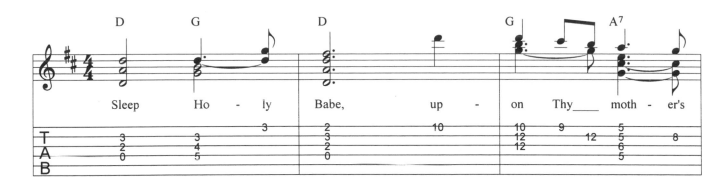

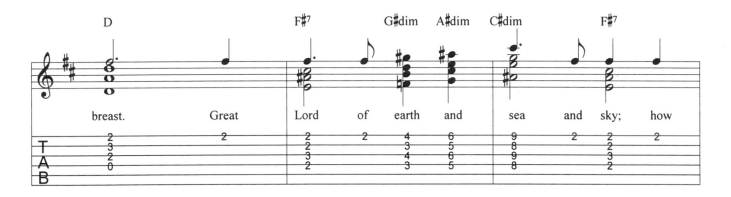

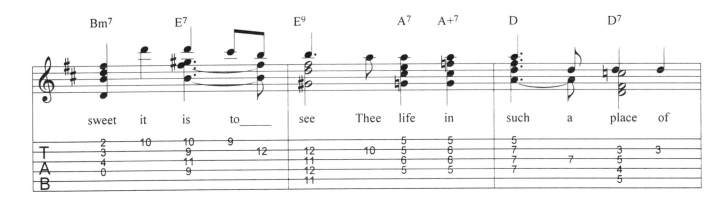

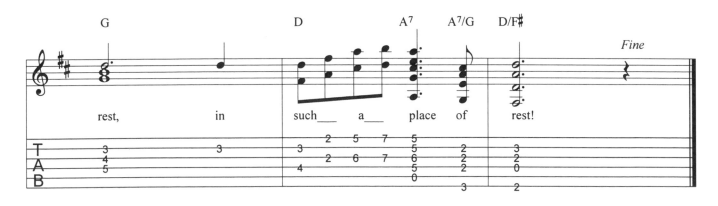

Sleep Holy Babe

(Intermediate)

Quietly

arr. by George Ports

Watchman, Tell Us Of The Night

(Easy)

Moderately

arr. by George Ports

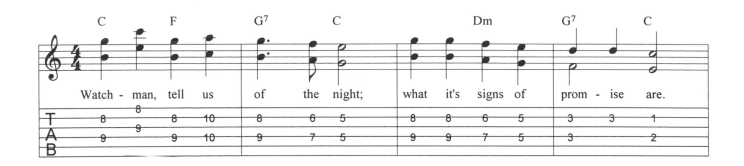

Watch - man, tell us of the night; what it's signs of prom - ise are.

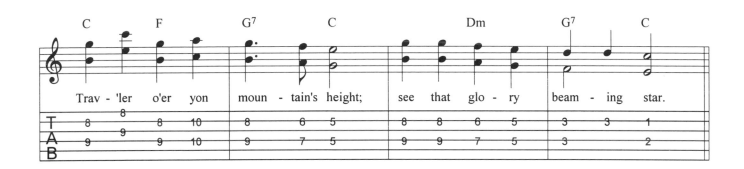

Trav - 'ler o'er yon moun - tain's height; see that glo - ry beam - ing star.

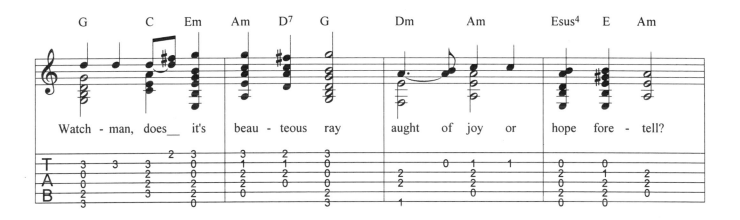

Watch - man, does it's beau - teous ray aught of joy or hope fore - tell?

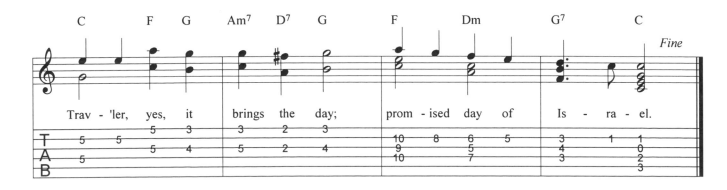

Trav - 'ler, yes, it brings the day; prom - ised day of Is - ra - el.

Watchman, Tell Us Of The Night

(Intermediate)

Moderately

arr. by George Ports

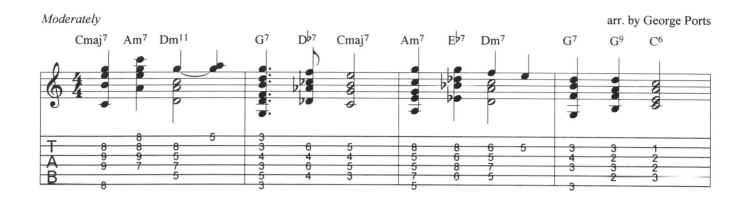

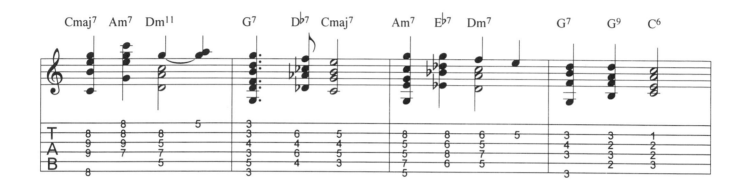

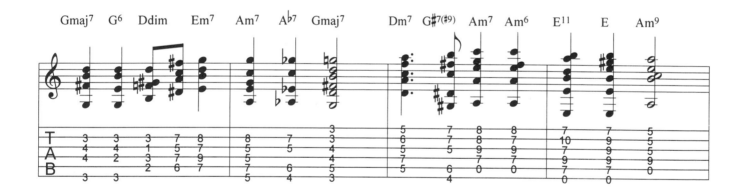

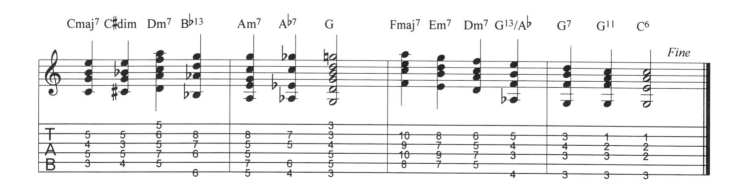

31